Way of the Cross

WAY OF THE CROSS

FOR LOVED ONES WHO HAVE LEFT THE FAITH

FR. JEFFREY KIRBY, STD

Our Sunday Visitor
Huntington, Indiana

Nihil Obstat
Msgr. Michael Heintz, Ph.D.
Censor Librorum

Imprimatur
✠ Kevin C. Rhoades
Bishop of Fort Wayne-South Bend
August 2, 2020

The *Nihil Obstat* and *Imprimatur* are official declarations that a book is free from doctrinal or moral error. It is not implied that those who have granted the *Nihil Obstat* and *Imprimatur* agree with the contents, opinions, or statements expressed.

Except where noted, the Scripture citations used in this work are taken from the *Revised Standard Version of the Bible — Second Catholic Edition* (Ignatius Edition), copyright © 1965, 1966, 2006 National Council of the Churches of Christ in the United States of America. Used by permission. All rights reserved.

Every reasonable effort has been made to determine copyright holders of excerpted materials and to secure permissions as needed. If any copyrighted materials have been inadvertently used in this work without proper credit being given in one form or another, please notify Our Sunday Visitor in writing so that future printings of this work may be corrected accordingly.

Copyright © 2021 by Fr. Jeffrey Kirby, STD

26 25 24 23 22 21   1 2 3 4 5 6 7 8 9

All rights reserved. With the exception of short excerpts for critical reviews, no part of this work may be reproduced or transmitted in any form or by any means whatsoever without permission from the publisher. For more information, visit: www.osv.com/permissions.

Our Sunday Visitor Publishing Division
Our Sunday Visitor, Inc.
200 Noll Plaza
Huntington, IN 46750
www.osv.com
1-800-348-2440

ISBN: 978-1-68192-675-9 (Inventory No. T2542)
1. RELIGION—Prayerbooks—Christian.
2. RELIGION—Holidays—Easter & Lent.
3. RELIGION—Christianity—Catholic.

eISBN: 978-1-68192-676-6
LCCN: 2020944379

Cover design: Tyler Ottinger
Cover/interior art: Stations of the Cross by Théophile Lybaert/Wiki Commons
Interior design: Amanda Falk

PRINTED IN THE UNITED STATES OF AMERICA

Dedicated to
Bishop Robert Baker, STD,
in gratitude for his apostolic witness

Introduction

OUR SORROW

Many of us have experienced the sorrow of having a loved one leave the Faith and abandon any semblance of its practice. For those of us who believe, there can be no greater heartache.

The reasons people have for leaving the Church are vast and varied. These reasons include anger with God over evil in the world; religious indifference; bad examples from believers; a contemporary thirst for material prosperity; disagreement with moral teachings; and the scandals in the Church.

Polls in the last few years have indicated that for every one convert to the Catholic Faith, we lose six members. So it shouldn't surprise us that of all the pastoral concerns in parish life, the most consistent and piercing sorrow is caused when loved ones walk away from the Faith.

The departure of so many from the Faith can be overwhelming. We can find ourselves caught up in an array of emotions, feeling helpless and unable to do anything. Conversations are cut short, dialogue is dismissed, and discussions are concluded with mockery. Believers seem to be hitting a wall. Arguments that have been studied and prepared are given no hearing or credence. Research intended to address various points of disagreement, and efforts at empathy with our loved ones, are drowned in apathy and callousness.

Are we helpless? Is there nothing we can do?

OUR HOPE

The Lord Jesus gives us hope. He also dealt with nonbelievers, and in his own heart he also suffered over the indifference of so many people who disregarded or mocked his offer of salvation. In all these scenarios, however, the Lord did not respond with self-pity, resentment, or accusation. Instead, the Lord responded with selfless love and compassion. In answer to the cold detachment of others, the Lord Jesus prayed, fasted, selflessly served, and offered up his immense sufferings for the good of those who ignored him. Even from the Cross, he prayed, "Father, forgive them; for they know not what they do" (Lk 23:34).

The offering of the Lord culminated in his Passion, Death, and Resurrection. In his torturous Passion, the Lord Jesus showed us the depth of his love. In carrying his Cross, he showed us the extent to which he would travel to reveal his kindness to us and share his friendship with us. The Lord sought our salvation beyond our negligence, and he loved us to the end.

In this way, the Lord Jesus modeled a noble response for us. By his self-oblation and desire for the salvation of all, the Lord exemplified and passed on to us his "most excellent way" of love (1 Cor 12:31). When we seek the return of our loved ones to the Faith, we are called to respond to them and generously offer them our prayers, selfless accompaniment, understanding, and compassion.

We are called to take the hard and often long road of loving others back into the consolation of faith and into the fold of the Church. This can be a difficult task, filled with good and bad moments. Through them all, however, and in spite of some of them, we are summoned to stay the course, persevere in hope, and pray tirelessly for the return of our loved ones.

As we accept the task of prayer, the Church offers some assistance.

A FITTING DEVOTION

As we contemplate the Lord's sacrificial love, the Church's beautiful and powerful devotion of the Stations of the Cross stands as a fitting response to the departure of loved ones from the Faith. The Stations allow us to take our concerns, heartache, and intercession before God the Father in the saving work of Jesus Christ. Each of us is able to walk with the Lord as he carries his Cross and to offer supplication for our loved ones.

As the Lord Jesus affectionately desires the salvation of all, so we are to unite ourselves with him in making supplication for our loved ones. Through the fourteen Stations of the Cross, we are able to intercede for our loved ones and spiritually carry the Cross with the Lord Jesus for their conversion back to fellowship with God and the Church.

As believers, we are not helpless. The Lord provides his grace, and the Church promotes the devotion of the Stations of the Cross for our benefit. It is fitting for us, therefore, to use this devotion for the swift return of our loved ones to the practice of the Faith.

THESE PARTICULAR STATIONS

Since this particular walk through the Stations of the Cross is written for our loved ones who have left the Faith, it will have a specific structure of prayers. Please note that each Station follows this format:

- *Traditional Opening.* Each Station begins with the traditional name of the Station and the prayer, "We adore you, O Christ …"
- *Scripture.* After the opening prayer, there is a small Bible passage that relates to the particular Station.
- *For Our Loved Ones.* After the Scripture reading, there is a prayer "For Our Loved Ones." This prayer applies the Station to the life of our loved ones and

expresses our concern and anxiety for those in our lives who do not have regular contact with God and his grace.

- *For Us.* After the prayer for our loved ones, there is a prayer "For Us." This is a petition for God to heal us from our pain and help us to become helpful instruments in bringing about the return of our loved ones. Oftentimes, in our supplication for loved ones, we can forget to ask God to strengthen us with the grace we need to be positive witnesses and models of the Christian way of life.

- *Closing Prayers.* Each Station ends with an Our Father, an Act of Faith, and a prayer to our guardian angels. These prayers are offered for both ourselves and our loved ones. Each Station also includes an optional personal prayer, particularly for

those who choose to pray these
Stations in private.

With the above explanation in mind, it's
time to turn our anxiety into prayer and
our frustration into supplication. It's time
to pray!

Opening Prayer

Leader: In the Name of the Father, and of the Son, and of the Holy Spirit. Amen.

Lord Jesus, you are the Mighty God and Prince of Peace.

You battle for our souls and labor for good to triumph in our fallen world. You are the Savior of souls and the Redeemer of humanity.

You walked the way of the Cross for

our salvation. You made the journey to die a bitter death, so that eternal life would be open to us.

In your way of the Cross, you showed us the immensity of your love. We thank you, Lord, and we seek the help of your grace. Help us to follow your way and to love you. We repent of our sins, and now we walk this sorrowful way with you.

As you have died for us, help us to die for you. Guide us to place all things under your Gospel and to trust you in all matters.

In particular, Lord, we make this way of the Cross today for our loved ones who have fallen away from you. We suffer by their absence, and we are burdened by their lack of faith.

But, in this way of the Cross, we surrender them to you.

Please help them, Lord. Use the grace of this sorrowful way to convert them and bring them back to you.

Lord Jesus, we trust in you!

And now, we begin our journey with you.

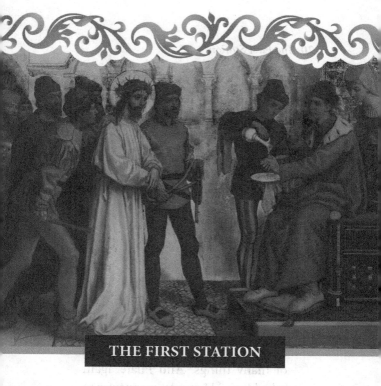

THE FIRST STATION

Jesus Is Condemned to Death

Leader: The First Station: Jesus Is Condemned to Death

(Genuflect)

We adore you, O Christ, and we praise you …

All: Because by your holy Cross you have redeemed the world.

(Stand)

Leader: We hear in the Sacred Scriptures:

> And the chief priests accused him of many things. And Pilate again asked him, "Have you no answer to make? See how many charges they bring against you." But Jesus made no further answer, so that Pilate wondered.
>
> Now at the feast he used to release for them one prisoner whom they asked. And among the rebels in prison, who had committed

murder in the insurrection, there was a man called Barabbas. And the crowd came up and began to ask Pilate to do as he was wont to do for them. And he answered them, "Do you want me to release for you the King of the Jews?" For he perceived that it was out of envy that the chief priests had delivered him up. But the chief priests stirred up the crowd to have him release for them Barabbas instead. And Pilate again said to them, "Then what shall I do with the man whom you call the King of the Jews?" And they cried out again, "Crucify him." And Pilate said to them, "Why, what evil has he done?" But they shouted all the more, "Crucify him." So Pilate, wishing to satisfy the crowd, released for them Barabbas; and having scourged Jesus, he delivered him to be crucified.

(Mark 15:3–15)

Leader: Let us pray. Lord Jesus, you allowed yourself to undergo trial and condemnation. In your human nature, you felt the fear of trusting in the Father's will, and yet you surrendered yourself completely to it. Although you prayed that the Father would remove the cup of suffering, you were prepared to drink it. You remained steadfast and had confidence in the goodness of the Father and his plan for our salvation.

Lord, our loved ones have many voices speaking to them. Many voices are calling the Father's goodness into question and raising doubts about the importance of his plan in their lives. You turned to the Father in the midst of unjust condemnation. We ask that you turn to our loved ones as they wrestle with their own trials and the condemnation of a life lived without you. Please bring them back to you. Give them the grace to trust in you and seek your fellowship in all they do. Bring them back to your Church.

(Kneel)

All: Lord, in your unjust condemnation, you sought the help of others, but they disappointed you. You asked your disciples for help and fellowship, but they neglected you and abandoned you. In our witness, we have also been negligent and distracted. At times, we have not gone the extra mile for our loved ones as they struggled with fear and doubt.

Lord, we ask you to help us. Show us how to be attentive and how to give a helpful witness to those who have fallen away from you. Help us to be your instruments of grace and peace to our loved ones. Lord, please bring our loved ones back to you and to your Church!

(Stand)

All: Our Father ...

Leader: We pray an Act of Faith for ourselves and our loved ones.

All: O my God, I firmly believe
that you are one God in three divine Persons,
Father, Son, and Holy Spirit.
I believe that your divine Son became man
and died for our sins and that he will come
to judge the living and the dead.
I believe these and all the truths
which the Holy Catholic Church teaches
because you have revealed them
who are eternal truth and wisdom,
who can neither deceive nor be deceived.
In this faith I intend to live and die.
Amen.

Leader: We ask the assistance of the holy angels in bringing our loved ones back to the Faith.

All: Angel of God, my guardian dear, to whom God's love commits me here. Ever this day be at my side, to light and guard, to rule and guide. Amen.

OPTIONAL PERSONAL PRAYER
Prayer for Guidance

By Henry Edward Cardinal Manning

O Holy Spirit of God, take me as your disciple; guide me, illuminate me, sanctify me. Bind my hands that they may do no evil; cover my eyes that they may see it no more; sanctify my heart that evil may not dwell within me. Be my God; be my Guide. Wherever you lead me, I will go; whatever you forbid me, I will renounce; and whatever you command me, in your strength, I will do. Lead me, then, unto the fullness of your truth. Amen.

THE SECOND STATION

Jesus Carries
His Cross

Leader: The Second Station: Jesus Carries His Cross

(Genuflect)

We adore you, O Christ, and we praise you ...

All: Because by your holy Cross you have redeemed the world.

(Stand)

Leader: We hear in the Sacred Scriptures:

> And the soldiers led [Jesus] away inside the palace (that is, the praetorium); and they called together the whole battalion. And they clothed him in a purple cloak, and plaiting a crown of thorns they put it on him. And they began to salute him, "Hail, King of the Jews!" And they struck his head with a reed, and spat upon him, and they knelt down in homage to him. And

when they had mocked him, they
stripped him of the purple cloak,
and put his own clothes on him.
And they led him out to crucify
him. (Mark 15:16–20)

Leader: Let us pray. Lord Jesus, you willingly
accepted the Cross. You faithfully carried it,
and by its weight you showed us the depth
of your love. In taking the Cross upon your
sacred shoulders, you displayed total trust in
the Father. Our world is fallen, and we are
a sinful people. There are many tribulations
and evils in life. By your Cross, O Lord, you
have vanquished them all and offered to us a
path of healing, salvation, and peace.

Lord Jesus, our loved ones have moved
away from you. They are not carrying their
crosses in life, but are being dragged about
by them. Without you and the help of your
grace, their crosses have no saving value.
They are overwhelmed, overburdened, and
heavy laden by the sin, hurt, and harm of
the world. The meaning, consolation, and
purpose of your Cross escapes them. As

you accepted your Cross, Lord Jesus, we ask that you turn to our loved ones and help them in carrying their crosses. Help them to see your presence and power in the midst of the darkness and disappointments of our fallen world. Please bring our loved ones back to you. Give them the grace to trust in you and seek your fellowship in all they do. Bring them back to your Church.

(Kneel)

All: Lord, in carrying your Cross, you modeled for us how we are to trust the Father and his care for us. At times, we have avoided our crosses and given bad witness to others. By our poor actions, we have not given testimony to the power of hope and of redemptive suffering in our world. By neglecting the Cross, we have missed many opportunities to allow grace to triumph over pride, mercy to heal sin, love to reconcile hurt, and peace to replace tension.

Lord, we ask you to help us. Show us how to faithfully carry our crosses and how

to be attentive to your grace in our lives.
Help us to be strong witnesses to the power
of the Cross in our world today, especially to our loved ones who have fallen away
from you. Lord, please bring our loved ones
back to you and to your Church!

(Stand)

All: Our Father …

Leader: We pray an Act of Faith for ourselves and our loved ones.

All: O my God, I firmly believe
that you are one God in three divine Persons,
Father, Son, and Holy Spirit.
I believe that your divine Son became man
and died for our sins and that he will come
to judge the living and the dead.
I believe these and all the truths
which the Holy Catholic Church teaches
because you have revealed them
who are eternal truth and wisdom,
who can neither deceive nor be deceived.

In this faith I intend to live and die.
Amen.

Leader: We ask the assistance of the holy angels in bringing our loved ones back to the Faith.

All: Angel of God, my guardian dear, to whom God's love commits me here. Ever this day be at my side, to light and guard, to rule and guide. Amen.

OPTIONAL PERSONAL PRAYER
Prayer of Resolution
Attributed to Saint Francis de Sales
O my God, henceforth, I resolve to strive earnestly to be patient and gentle, and not allow the waters of contradiction to extinguish the fire of charity which I owe to my neighbor.
Amen.

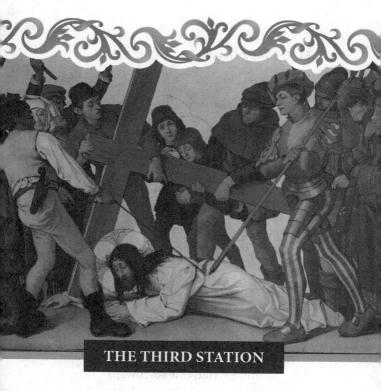

THE THIRD STATION

Jesus Falls the
First Time

Leader: The Third Station: Jesus Falls the First Time

(Genuflect)

We adore you, O Christ, and we praise you …

All: Because by your holy Cross you have redeemed the world.

(Stand)

Leader: We hear in the Sacred Scriptures:

> Surely he has borne our griefs
>   and carried our sorrows;
> yet we esteemed him stricken,
>   struck down by God, and af-
>   flicted.
> But he was wounded for our trans-
>   gressions,
>   he was bruised for our iniqui-
>   ties;
> upon him was the chastisement
>   that made us whole,

and with his stripes we are
healed.
All we like sheep have gone astray;
we have turned every one to
his own way;
and the LORD has laid on him
the iniquity of us all.
(Isaiah 53:4–6)

Leader: Let us pray. Lord Jesus, in carrying the Cross, you fell three times. The weight of the beam and the fatigue of your human nature overpowered your own human strength, and you succumbed to utter exhaustion. Your body and soul felt the weight of our fallen world. You understand the heaviness of our sinful world and the weight that is often placed upon us by the sufferings and struggles of life.

Lord Jesus, our loved ones have fallen under the weight of this world. They have left the Cross of faith and decline to live by its promises. Without faith, they cannot know you or truly know others. Without faith, the fallenness of suspicion, anxiety, and distrust have taken their hearts. They have fallen, Lord, and they need you. As you fell under the weight of the Cross, we ask that you meet our loved ones there — under the Cross. Give them again the grace of faith and the joy of knowing and loving you. Please, Lord, bring our loved ones back to you. Give them the grace to trust in you and seek your fellowship in all they do. Bring them back to your Church.

(Kneel)

All: Lord, in your first fall, you showed us that you have a perfect knowledge of all our truly human experiences. You loved with a human heart, cried with human tears, and worked with human hands. You knew thirst and grief. You suffered. In all these ways, you seek to save us from the inside out. You have walked this human way of life and have shown us how to live as the children of God. You are the faithful Friend and Companion to the human family. You are a gentle Confidant to us and to our loved ones. In our pride, resentment, and self-pity, we have not imitated your kindness to those who have struggled to accept you, or to those who have left the Faith. We have allowed judgment to replace love.

Lord, we ask you to help us. Show us how to repent of our own fallenness and to love those who have fallen away from you. Help us to be gentle companions, to speak the truth in love, and to show our love through patience and kindness. Lord, please bring our loved ones back to you and to your Church!

(Stand)

All: Our Father …

Leader:
We pray an Act of Faith for ourselves and our loved ones.

All: O my God, I firmly believe
that you are one God in three divine Persons,

Father, Son, and Holy Spirit.
I believe that your divine Son became man
and died for our sins and that he will come
to judge the living and the dead.
I believe these and all the truths
which the Holy Catholic Church teaches
because you have revealed them
who are eternal truth and wisdom,
who can neither deceive nor be deceived.
In this faith I intend to live and die.
Amen.

Leader: We ask the assistance of the holy angels in bringing our loved ones back to the Faith.

All: Angel of God, my guardian dear, to whom God's love commits me here. Ever this day be at my side, to light and guard, to rule and guide. Amen.

OPTIONAL PERSONAL PRAYER
Prayer of the Angel at Fatima
My God,
I believe,
I adore,
I hope,
and I love You!
I ask pardon of You for those
who do not believe,
do not adore,
do not hope,
and do not love You!
Amen.

THE FOURTH STATION

Jesus Meets
His Mother

Leader: The Fourth Station: Jesus Meets His Mother

(Genuflect)

We adore you, O Christ, and we praise you …

All: Because by your holy Cross you have redeemed the world.

(Stand)

Leader: We hear in the Sacred Scriptures:

> "Behold, this child is set for the fall
>   and rising of many in
>   Israel,
> and for a sign that will be spoken
>   against
> (and a sword will pierce through
>   your own soul also),
> that thoughts out of many
>   hearts may be revealed."
>   (Luke 2:34–35)

Leader: Let us pray. Lord Jesus, along the way of the Cross, you met your mother. What grief filled your own heart, as she saw you and cried for you. What heaviness was yours, as your mother shared in your agony. The sight of your own mother, your own flesh and blood, enduring your bitter Passion with you, consumed your soul with great sadness.

Lord Jesus, you carry our loved ones in your heart. As they have left the practice of the Faith, you continue to suffer in their indifference and mockery. As our loved ones walk this world and experience its joys and sorrows, they do not recognize that you are with them. As you suffer in them, so let us imitate Mary and share in your agony. As you were consoled by the presence and tenderness of your mother, so let our loved ones know of our companionship and faithfulness. Let our love be a way to bring them back to the Faith. Let love triumph. Please, Lord, bring our loved ones back to you. Give them the grace to trust in you and seek your fellowship in all they do.

Bring them back to your Church.
(Kneel)

All: Lord, in meeting your mother along the way of the Cross, you showed us the importance of family and friendship. You were consoled by the warmth of such a blessed encounter. You were inspired by her spiritual accompaniment. Throughout your Passion, your mother was with you and walked with you. Your sufferings were her sufferings, and your Cross was her Cross. Often in our hard-heartedness, we have not met you in the lives of our loved ones who have left the Faith. We have not offered you consolation, as you work within their hearts.

Lord, we ask you to help us. Show us how to welcome and accompany you in those who are away from the Faith. Help us to be true mother, brother, and sister to you. Lord, please bring our loved ones back to you and to your Church!

(Stand)

All: Our Father …

Leader: We pray an Act of Faith for ourselves and our loved ones.

All: O my God, I firmly believe
that you are one God in three divine Persons,
Father, Son, and Holy Spirit.
I believe that your divine Son became man
and died for our sins and that he will come
to judge the living and the dead.
I believe these and all the truths
which the Holy Catholic Church teaches
because you have revealed them
who are eternal truth and wisdom,
who can neither deceive nor be deceived.
In this faith I intend to live and die.
Amen.

Leader: We ask the assistance of the holy angels in bringing our loved ones back to the Faith.

All: Angel of God, my guardian dear, to whom God's love commits me here. Ever

this day be at my side, to light and guard, to rule and guide. Amen.

OPTIONAL PERSONAL PRAYER
Memorare

Remember, O most gracious Virgin Mary, that never was it known that anyone who fled to your protection, implored your assistance, or sought your intercession was left unaided. Inspired by this confidence, we fly unto you, O Virgin of Virgins, our Mother. To you we come, before you we kneel, sinful and sorrowful. O Mother of the Word Incarnate, despise not our petitions, but in your clemency, hear and answer them.

Amen.

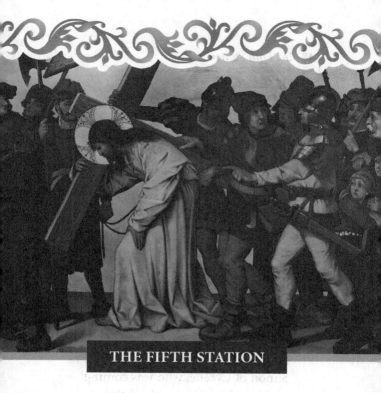

Simon of Cyrene Helps Jesus Carry His Cross

Leader: The Fifth Station: Simon of Cyrene Helps Jesus Carry His Cross

(Genuflect)

We adore you, O Christ, and we praise you …

All: Because by your holy Cross you have redeemed the world.

(Stand)

Leader: We hear in the Sacred Scriptures:

> And they compelled a passer-by, Simon of Cyrene, who was coming in from the country, the father of Alexander and Rufus, to carry his cross. And they brought him to the place called Golgotha (which means the place of a skull).
>
> (Mark 15:21–22)

Leader: Let us pray. Lord Jesus, Simon of Cyrene was sent to help you carry the weight of your Cross. He lightened the heaviness of its beam and did not add any weight to it. It was an unexpected relief to your burdens. Simon held no judgment toward you. There was no unkindness or mockery. The encounter was encouraging and without shame.

Lord Jesus, you welcomed Simon's help. You needed it as the Cross pushed you beyond the limits of your human nature. He came as a companion and shared in your disgrace. Lord, as our loved ones carry their various crosses in this world, which are heightened by their absence from you, please do not be a stranger to them. Turn to our loved ones in their struggles and disbelief, and be a Simon of Cyrene to them. Let them know of your love and strength. Please, Lord, be their help. Be a Companion to them as they endure the sufferings of this life. Bring our loved ones back to you. Give them the grace to trust in you and to seek your fellowship in all they do. Bring them back to your Church.

(Kneel)

All: Lord, in receiving the assistance of Simon of Cyrene, you revealed to us the power of selfless accompaniment. You were greatly aided by the strength of another. Lord, you humbled yourself and accepted help. You were encouraged by the act of kindness. By his aid, Simon was a consolation and joy to you. He carried a portion of the weight of your own Cross. In our pride, we have allowed selfish intentions to overtake our efforts to help those who are away from you. We have allowed our own pain, grief, and embarrassment to darken our desire to help carry the crosses of others.

Lord, we ask you to help us. Show us how to be like Simon of Cyrene to those who have walked away from you. Help us to selflessly accompany others and how to graciously help them carry their crosses. Lord, please bring our loved ones back to you and to your Church!

(Stand)

All: Our Father ...

Leader: We pray an Act of Faith for ourselves and our loved ones.

All: O my God, I firmly believe
that you are one God in three divine Persons,
Father, Son, and Holy Spirit.
I believe that your divine Son became man
and died for our sins and that he will come
to judge the living and the dead.
I believe these and all the truths
which the Holy Catholic Church teaches
because you have revealed them
who are eternal truth and wisdom,
who can neither deceive nor be deceived.
In this faith I intend to live and die.
Amen.

Leader: We ask the assistance of the holy angels in bringing our loved ones back to the Faith.

All: Angel of God, my guardian dear, to whom God's love commits me here. Ever

this day be at my side, to light and guard, to rule and guide. Amen.

OPTIONAL PERSONAL PRAYER
Prayer of Self-Surrender
Attributed to Saint Ignatius of Loyola
Take, Lord, and receive all my liberty,
my memory, my understanding,
and my entire will,
all I have and call my own.

You have given all to me.
To you, Lord, I return it.

Everything is yours; do
with it what you will.
Give me only your love and your grace.
That is enough for me.

Amen.

THE SIXTH STATION

Veronica Wipes
the Face of Jesus

Leader: The Sixth Station: Veronica Wipes the Face of Jesus

(Genuflect)

We adore you, O Christ, and we praise you …

All: Because by your holy Cross you have redeemed the world.

(Stand)

Leader: We hear in the Sacred Scriptures:

> Then the righteous will answer him, "Lord, when did we see you hungry and feed you, or thirsty and give you drink? And when did we see you a stranger and welcome you, or naked and clothe you? And when did we see you sick or in prison and visit you?" And the King will answer them, "Truly, I say to you, as you did it to one of the least of these my brethren, you

did it to me." (Matthew 25:37–40)

Leader: Let us pray. Lord Jesus, in contrast to the offenses of so many, the holy woman Veronica gave you soothing and heartfelt care as she wiped the sweat and blood from your face in the midst of your Passion. The woman's surprising act of kindness was a consoling break from the brutality and harshness of your Cross. As others mocked you and reviled you, Veronica offered you only compassion and understanding.

Lord Jesus, you accepted Veronica's care. You were comforted by her goodwill and innocent affection toward you. While so many bystanders only saw a criminal to scorn, Veronica saw a fellow human being in need of help and attention. She did not delay, but quickly came to your assistance. Lord, as our loved ones endure a life without you or the consolation of your grace, send Veronicas to them. Please see their sorrows and scars and quickly turn to them. Give them the solace and encouragement of your love and mercy.

Let them know your presence and tenderness. Lord, please bring our loved ones back to you. Give them the grace to trust in you and seek your fellowship in all they do. Bring them back to your Church.

(Kneel)

All: Lord, in receiving the benevolence of Veronica, you disclosed to us the meekness and humility of your own heart. There was no pride or defensiveness in you. In this gracious encounter, you were open and docile to the help of another. Veronica was a surprise blessing to you. In our fallenness, however, we have approached others in a spirit of scorn or dismissiveness. We have lacked the gentleness and kindness of Veronica. We have allowed a spirit of judgment and vainglory to distract us from your call to patience and selfless service toward those who are away from you.

Lord, we ask you to help us. Show us how to be like Veronica to those who have abandoned your way of love. Help us to be gracious and to wash the face of those who need you. Lord, please bring our loved ones back to you and to your Church!

(Stand)

All: Our Father ...

Leader: We pray an Act of Faith for ourselves and our loved ones.

All: O my God, I firmly believe
that you are one God in three divine Persons,
Father, Son, and Holy Spirit.
I believe that your divine Son became man
and died for our sins and that he will come
to judge the living and the dead.
I believe these and all the truths
which the Holy Catholic Church teaches
because you have revealed them
who are eternal truth and wisdom,
who can neither deceive nor be deceived.
In this faith I intend to live and die.
Amen.

Leader: We ask the assistance of the holy angels in bringing our loved ones back to the Faith.

All: Angel of God, my guardian dear, to whom God's love commits me here. Ever this day be at my side, to light and guard, to rule and guide. Amen.

OPTIONAL PERSONAL PRAYER
Soul of Christ

Soul of Christ, sanctify me.
Body of Christ, save me.
Blood of Christ, inebriate me.
Water from the side of Christ, wash me.
Passion of Christ, strengthen me.
O good Jesus, hear me.
Within your wounds, hide me.
Never let me be separated from you.
From the malignant enemy, defend me.
At the hour of death, call me;
and bid me come to you.
That with your saints I may praise you
forever and ever.
Amen.

THE SEVENTH STATION

Jesus Falls the
Second Time

Leader: The Seventh Station: Jesus Falls the Second Time

(Genuflect)

We adore you, O Christ, and we praise you …

All: Because by your holy Cross you have redeemed the world.

(Stand)

Leader: We hear in the Sacred Scriptures:

> All nations surrounded me;
> in the name of the LORD I cut
> them off!
> They surrounded me, surrounded
> me on every side;
> in the name of the LORD I cut
> them off!
> They surrounded me like bees,
> they blazed like a fire of thorns;
> in the name of the LORD I cut
> them off!

I was pushed hard, so that I was
falling,
but the Lord helped me.
The Lord is my strength and my
song;
he has become my salvation.
(Psalm 118:10–14)

Leader: Let us pray. Lord Jesus, your Cross was overwhelming. Its weight knocked you down a second time. As you struggled to complete the mission given to you by the Father, your body was breaking, and you couldn't walk. Your soul was heavy, burdened with the sins and sorrows of humanity. And you accepted this bitterness of body and soul because of your love for the Father and for each of us. You focused only on the saving mission given to you.

Lord Jesus, our loved ones have fallen under the burdens of this world. They have refused your Cross. They avoid it and the hope that comes with it. Without such hope, they cannot trust you or see your ways. And without a firm trust in you, they cannot truly trust others. Without hope, their hearts are susceptible to the pain of desolation, distrust, and despair. They have fallen, Lord, and they need you. As you fell under the weight of the Cross, we ask that you meet our loved ones there — under the Cross. Give them the grace of hope and strengthen their trust in you. Please, Lord, bring our loved ones back to you. Give them the grace to trust in you and seek your fellowship in all they do. Bring them back to your Church.

(Kneel)

All: Lord, in your second fall, you showed us how deeply you desire to accompany us and be with us through the sorrows and sufferings of life. You understand disappointment and hurt. You also know betrayal. Because you know the fallenness of the world and the sorrows of our hearts, you walk with us and offer us hope. Hope points us to eternity and reveals to us the face of our Father. Hope gives us confidence. It brings light to darkness and shows us that sin and death do not have the last word. Hope gives us victory and saves us from the darkness of our fallen world. Lord, you are our only Hope. You are the Light of the world, the Morning Dawn, and the Beginning and End of all things. In our hurt, we have refused to remember the fallenness of our loved ones, and how their brokenness has drawn them away from you. We have allowed self-righteousness and self-pity to weigh us down.

Lord, we ask you to help us. Fill us with repentance for our own fallenness and open our hearts to accept the hope that you offer to all men and women. Help us to see all things from the light of eternity and to trust in your compassion for our loved ones who are away from you. Strengthen us! Help us to be joyful in hope, patient in suffering, and faithful in prayer. Lord, please bring our loved ones back to you and to your Church!

(Stand)

All: Our Father …

Leader: We pray an Act of Faith for ourselves and our loved ones.

All: O my God, I firmly believe
that you are one God in three divine Persons,
Father, Son, and Holy Spirit.
I believe that your divine Son became man
and died for our sins and that he will come
to judge the living and the dead.
I believe these and all the truths
which the Holy Catholic Church teaches
because you have revealed them
who are eternal truth and wisdom,
who can neither deceive nor be deceived.
In this faith I intend to live and die.
Amen.

Leader: We ask the assistance of the holy angels in bringing our loved ones back to the Faith.

All: Angel of God, my guardian dear, to whom God's love commits me here. Ever

this day be at my side, to light and guard, to rule and guide. Amen.

OPTIONAL PERSONAL PRAYER
Act of Hope
O my God, relying on Your almighty power and infinite mercy and promises, I hope to obtain pardon of my sins, the help of Your grace and life everlasting, through the merits of Jesus Christ, my Lord and Redeemer.
Amen.

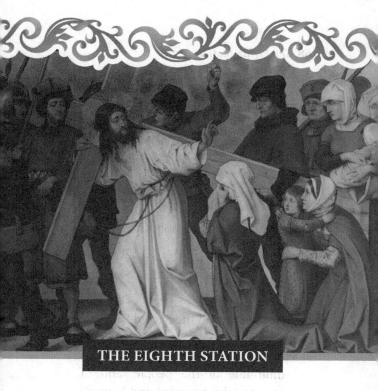

Jesus Comforts the Holy Women of Jerusalem

Leader: The Eighth Station: Jesus Comforts the Holy Women of Jerusalem

(Genuflect)

We adore you, O Christ, and we praise you ...

All: Because by your holy Cross you have redeemed the world.

(Stand)

Leader: We hear in the Sacred Scriptures:

> And there followed him a great multitude of the people, and of women who bewailed and lamented him. But Jesus turning to them said, "Daughters of Jerusalem, do not weep for me, but weep for yourselves and for your children. For behold, the days are coming when they will say, 'Blessed are the barren, and the wombs that never bore, and the breasts that never nursed!' Then

> they will begin to say to the moun-
> tains, 'Fall on us'; and to the hills,
> 'Cover us.' For if they do this when
> the wood is green, what will happen
> when it is dry?"
>
> (Luke 23:27–31)

Leader: Let us pray. Lord Jesus, as you carried your Cross, many mocked and jeered
at you. A group of holy women, however,
shared in your sorrows. They saw your suffering, and they cried for you and wailed
over your sufferings and rejection. In contrast to the judgment and denunciations of
others, the holy women acknowledged you,
commiserated with the bitterness of your
Passion, and showed a loving kindness toward you. Their empathy was a solace and
comfort to you as you showed us your love
and faithfully carried your Cross.

Lord Jesus, our loved ones carry so
many crosses in this fallen world. They
think they can handle everything alone.
They falsely believe that they are the sole
standard of what it means to be good. They

only accept their own self-written narrative. Such a worldview is small. It cheats our loved ones of the immensity of your love and the broad horizon given to us by faith. Lord, as the holy women cried and wailed for you, please show compassion to our loved ones and shed holy tears for them. Let them know of your love and tenderness. Please, Lord, bring our loved ones back to you. Give them the grace to trust in you and seek your fellowship in all they do. Bring them back to your Church.

(Kneel)

All: Lord, as the holy women grieved for you, you received their act of kindness; but you also called them to mourn over their own children. You summoned them to greater acts of prayer and compassion. In this way, you showed us the inner depth of your Sacred Heart and the selfless nature of your love. You asked the holy women to give to others what they were offering to you. Your attention was always on others and never on yourself. In this way, you reveal to us the interior spirit of the way of the Cross. It is the path of humility, selfless love, and generosity of heart. Lord, you want us to follow this way. You call us to show kindness to each other and to take care of one another. And yet, we disappoint you. We neglect those in need; we judge those who are away from you; and we close our hearts to those who are suffering.

Lord, we ask you to help us. Fill us with sorrow and bless us with holy tears. Help us to grieve over the evil of our world and to wail over the hurts and sorrows of our loved ones. Lord, please soften our hearts! Help us to be gracious in our empathy, generous in our kindness, and welcoming to those who are away from you. Lord, please bring our loved ones back to you and to your Church!

(Stand)

All: Our Father …

Leader: We pray an Act of Faith for ourselves and our loved ones.

All: O my God, I firmly believe
that you are one God in three divine Persons,
Father, Son, and Holy Spirit.
I believe that your divine Son became man
and died for our sins and that he will come
to judge the living and the dead.
I believe these and all the truths
which the Holy Catholic Church teaches
because you have revealed them
who are eternal truth and wisdom,
who can neither deceive nor be deceived.
In this faith I intend to live and die.
Amen.

Leader: We ask the assistance of the holy
angels in bringing our loved ones back to
the Faith.

All: Angel of God, my guardian dear, to
whom God's love commits me here. Ever
this day be at my side, to light and guard, to
rule and guide. Amen.

OPTIONAL PERSONAL PRAYER
Hail, Holy Queen

Hail, Holy Queen, Mother of mercy,
our life, our sweetness and our hope.
To thee do we cry, poor banished children of Eve:
to thee do we send up our sighs,
mourning and weeping in this valley of tears.
Turn then, most gracious Advocate,
thine eyes of mercy toward us,
and after this, our exile,
show unto us the blessed fruit of thy womb, Jesus.
O clement, O loving, O sweet Virgin Mary!
Amen.

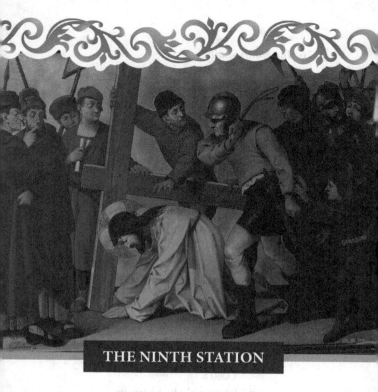

THE NINTH STATION

Jesus Falls the Third Time

Leader: The Ninth Station: Jesus Falls the Third Time

(Genuflect)

We adore you, O Christ, and we praise you …

All: Because by your holy Cross you have redeemed the world.

(Stand)

Leader: We hear in the Sacred Scriptures:

> The steps of a man are from the
>   LORD,
>   and he establishes him in
>   whose way he delights;
> though he fall, he shall not be cast
>   headlong,
>   for the LORD is the stay of
>   his hand.
>   (Psalm 37:23–24)

Leader: Let us pray. Lord Jesus, on the way

of the Cross, you fell three times. And while the weight of our sins threw you down, your love for us lifted you up. As you neared the end of your journey to Calvary, this third fall was the worst. Your body was completely drained and your soul was spent. With your fall, so many ridiculed and sneered at you. In spite of such mistreatment and indifference, you raised your Cross again. You responded to offense, debasement, and ingratitude with an unlimited and sweeping love. You did not let animosity overpower you. You lifted your Cross for a third time so that darkness would be destroyed and love would triumph.

Lord Jesus, our loved ones suffer under the fallenness of our world. They have abandoned your Cross and the most excellent way of love that it exemplifies for us. Without your love, we cannot know how to selflessly love others. Without the Cross, love discards suffering and demands rewards, comfort, and luxury. Without the cross, we become self-absorbed and our love becomes selfish. Lord, our loved ones have fallen, and they need your witness of self-less love to rise again. As you fell under the weight of the Cross, we ask that you meet our loved ones there — under the Cross — and give them again the power and grace of love to empty themselves in service to others. Please, Lord, bring our loved ones back to you. Give them the grace to trust in you and seek your fellowship in all they do. Bring them back to your Church.

(Kneel)

All: Lord, in your third fall, you showed us the depth of your love. You became a man of sorrows who knew rejection, indifference, and offense. Yet you continued to pour yourself out in compassion and service to others, even to those who mocked you or ignored you. In your third fall, the world sees your woundedness. Though wounded, you did not stop loving. Even now, in the midst of our transgressions against you, you generously offer us your love. You call us to yourself and reveal to us your Sacred Heart.

Love directs us to give of ourselves; it shows us who we are and what we are called to be. Love brings warmth to coldness, meaning to uncertainty, and relationship to loneliness. Lord, you are Love. You are the True Vine, the Living Bread, and the Good Shepherd. In our own woundedness, we have not followed your way of love. We have been easily offended and have turned away from our loved ones who have turned away from you — especially when they have hurt us. We have used their offenses as excuses and have not carried the Cross of self-emptying love.

Lord, we ask you to help us. We repent. Open our hearts to accept the love that you offer to all. Assist us in loving others beyond self-pity and entitlement. Guide us in your way of selfless love. In our woundedness, restore us and help us to love you and our loved ones more deeply. Lord, please bring our loved ones back to you and to your Church!

(Stand)

All: Our Father …

Leader: We pray an Act of Faith for ourselves and our loved ones.

All: O my God, I firmly believe
that you are one God in three divine Persons,
Father, Son, and Holy Spirit.
I believe that your divine Son became man
and died for our sins and that he will come
to judge the living and the dead.
I believe these and all the truths
which the Holy Catholic Church teaches
because you have revealed them
who are eternal truth and wisdom,
who can neither deceive nor be deceived.
In this faith I intend to live and die.
Amen.

Leader: We ask the assistance of the holy angels in bringing our loved ones back to the Faith.

All: Angel of God, my guardian dear, to whom God's love commits me here. Ever

this day be at my side, to light and guard, to rule and guide. Amen.

**OPTIONAL PERSONAL PRAYER
Act of Love**
O my God, I love you above all things, with my whole heart and soul, because you are all good and worthy of all my love. I love my neighbor as myself for the love of you. I forgive all who have injured me, and I ask pardon of all whom I have injured. Through Christ our Lord. Amen.

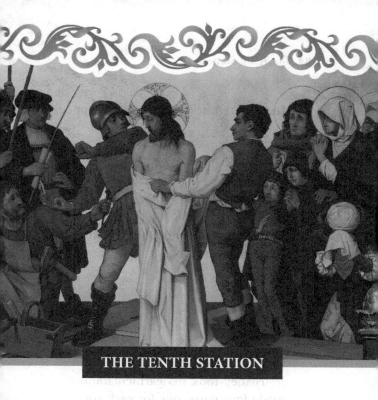

THE TENTH STATION

Jesus Is Stripped
of His Garments

Leader: The Tenth Station: Jesus Is Stripped of His Garments

(Genuflect)

We adore you, O Christ, and we praise you …

All: Because by your holy Cross you have redeemed the world.

(Stand)

Leader: We hear in the Sacred Scriptures:

> When the soldiers had crucified Jesus they took his garments and made four parts, one for each soldier; also his tunic. But the tunic was without seam, woven from top to bottom; so they said to one another, "Let us not tear it, but cast lots for it to see whose it shall be." This was to fulfil the Scripture, "They parted my garments among them, and for my clothing they cast

lots." (John 19:23–24)

Leader: Let us pray. Lord Jesus, on reaching Calvary, the soldiers humiliated you by stripping you of your clothes and casting lots for them. They dismissed your dignity and treated you as a commodity. In response to such abasement, you remained silent. Your body was crushed and mangled, bruised and bloody. You sought no consolation and brought every offense into the work of our redemption. Stripped of your clothes, you were ridiculed in your nakedness and scorned in your vulnerability. Despite such treatment, you retained your dignity, preserved your nobility of purpose, and cherished the saving mission entrusted to you by the Father. Lord, you allowed nothing to distract you or discourage you. You were at the place of sacrifice and you were ready.

Lord Jesus, our loved ones have stripped themselves of your protection and grace. They are spiritually naked and defenseless. They have removed the garments of your love and mercy. Sin seeks to define them and give them the false clothing of pride and arrogance. They remain naked, but they think they are clothed. Open their eyes, Lord. Help them to see where they stand and how helpless they are. Please show them the true dangers of a world that refuses to live by your virtues of love, humility, and self-control. Help them to be clothed in your goodness and righteousness. Please, Lord, bring our loved ones back to you. Give them the grace to trust in you and seek your fellowship in all they do. Bring them back to your Church.

(Kneel)

All: Lord, as you were stripped of your clothing, you manifested your dignity and nobility to the world. In this action, you showed us our own dignity and called us to follow you. You approached Calvary with docility toward the Father and kindness toward each of us. You were publicly shamed and treated as a criminal, though you bore no fault and had committed no crime. You allowed yourself to be a prisoner and tortured. You allowed yourself to be derided and humiliated. You could have called on legions of angels to protect you, but you stood vulnerable and accepted the injustice, the falls, and the stripping of your clothes. You resigned yourself to these offenses because they have become the means of our salvation. By your stripes, we are healed. Lord, in our defensiveness, we have not accepted humiliations from others, especially those who are away from you. We have reacted harshly, denounced others, and refused to stand naked and vulnerable in our witness to you. We have forgotten the power of suffering and denied your way of humility.

Lord, we ask you to help us. We are sorrowful and heavyhearted. We wish the best for our loved ones and we want them to be with you. We are vulnerable and hurting, naked and helpless. Guide us in your way of humility. Help us to clothe ourselves in you, and to love others in spite of humiliation! Lord, please bring our loved ones back to you and to your Church!

(Stand)

All: Our Father …

Leader: We pray an Act of Faith for ourselves and our loved ones.

All: O my God, I firmly believe
that you are one God in three divine Persons,
Father, Son, and Holy Spirit.
I believe that your divine Son became man
and died for our sins and that he will come
to judge the living and the dead.
I believe these and all the truths
which the Holy Catholic Church teaches
because you have revealed them
who are eternal truth and wisdom,
who can neither deceive nor be deceived.
In this faith I intend to live and die.
Amen.

Leader: We ask the assistance of the holy angels in bringing our loved ones back to the Faith.

All: Angel of God, my guardian dear, to whom God's love commits me here. Ever this day be at my side, to light and guard, to rule and guide. Amen.

OPTIONAL PERSONAL PRAYER
Litany of Humility
Attributed to Cardinal
Rafael Merry del Val
O Jesus, meek and humble of heart,
> *Hear me.*
From the desire of being esteemed,
> *Deliver me, Jesus.*
From the desire of being loved,
> *Deliver me, Jesus.*
From the desire of being extolled,
> *Deliver me, Jesus.*
From the desire of being honored,
> *Deliver me, Jesus.*
From the desire of being praised,
> *Deliver me, Jesus.*
From the desire of being preferred to others,

Deliver me, Jesus.
From the desire of being consulted,
Deliver me, Jesus.
From the desire of being approved,
Deliver me, Jesus.
From the fear of being humiliated,
Deliver me, Jesus.
From the fear of being despised,
Deliver me, Jesus.
From the fear of suffering rebukes,
Deliver me, Jesus.
From the fear of being calumniated,
Deliver me, Jesus.
From the fear of being forgotten,
Deliver me, Jesus.
From the fear of being ridiculed,
Deliver me, Jesus.
From the fear of being wronged,
Deliver me, Jesus.
From the fear of being suspected,
Deliver me, Jesus.

That others may be loved more than I,
>   *Jesus, grant me the grace to desire it.*

That others may be esteemed more than I,
>   *Jesus, grant me the grace to desire it.*

That in the opinion of the world, others may increase, and I may decrease,
>   *Jesus, grant me the grace to desire it.*

That others may be chosen and I set aside,
>   *Jesus, grant me the grace to desire it.*

That others may be praised and I unnoticed,
>   *Jesus, grant me the grace to desire it.*

That others may be preferred to me in everything,
>   *Jesus, grant me the grace to desire it.*

That others may become holier than I, provided that I become as holy as I should,
>   *Jesus, grant me the grace to desire it.*

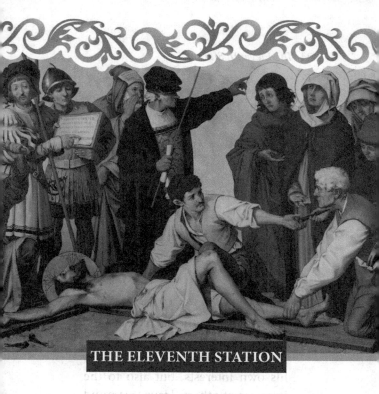

Jesus Is Nailed
to the Cross

Leader: The Eleventh Station: Jesus Is Nailed to the Cross

(Genuflect)

We adore you, O Christ, and we praise you …

All: Because by your holy Cross you have redeemed the world.

(Stand)

Leader: We hear in the Sacred Scriptures:

> Let each of you look not only to his own interests, but also to the interests of others. Have this mind among yourselves, which was in Christ Jesus, who, though he was in the form of God, did not count equality with God a thing to be grasped, but emptied himself, taking the form of a servant, being born in the likeness of men. And being found in human form he

> humbled himself and became obe-
> dient unto death, even death on a
> cross. (Philippians 2:4–8)

Leader: Let us pray. Lord Jesus, after being stripped of your clothing, you were thrown down and brutally nailed to the Cross. There was no gentleness, no pause, and no compassion. It was stark and merciless. Your hands and your feet were barbarously intruded by raw nails. The pain was unimaginable. The scene was savage and inhumane. And yet, your love triumphed. You responded to such ruthlessness with humility and tranquility of spirit. In the anguish of these moments, you thought of nothing but us and of your mission to save us from the sin and darkness of this world.

Lord Jesus, our loved ones are enduring a brutality of spirit. Without your presence, our fallen world is nailing them to the wall. It gives them no mercy or compassion. It offers no second chances. It eats them up and spits them out. They are forced to grovel before the vainglory and greed of our age. They have no rock, no foundation, and no reason for hope. But we were not made for such slavery. As you were nailed to the Cross, Lord, you understood this harshness and its crushing assault on the human soul. Please turn to our loved ones and call them back to you. Show them the power of your mercy and the hope of new beginnings. Please, Lord, bring our loved ones back to you. Give them the grace to trust in you and seek your fellowship in all they do. Bring them back to your Church.

(Kneel)

All: Lord, as the nails pierced your sacred flesh, you suffered their torment and experienced their excruciating pain. The nails are symbols of our sins, which led you to the Cross, just as they are symbols of your love, which vanquished sin and darkness forever. In accepting the nails, you proved to us the immensity of your love for each of us, especially those who are far from you. In the throes of ruthless torture, you triumphed with goodness. You did not respond with evil, but unleashed the power of your grace. Your goodness and innocence eradicated evil and dispelled darkness for all ages. You are our Savior and Friend, Lord and Companion. But, Lord, we have not followed you. We have avoided suffering and have refused the nails of love. We have strayed from you by indulging in rash judgment, negativity, and resentment. We have allowed the hurt and harm that has been done to us to justify our grudges, our annoyances, and our malice.

Lord, we ask you to help us. We repent of our offenses. Show us the wounds in your hands and heart. Convict us to open our hearts to greater mercy and compassion. Guide us along the path of your love. Give us your grace. Help us to respond to evil with goodness, and to harshness with gentleness. Lord, please bring our loved ones back to you and to your Church!

(Stand)

All: Our Father ...

Leader: We pray an Act of Faith for ourselves and our loved ones.

All: O my God, I firmly believe
that you are one God in three divine Persons,
Father, Son, and Holy Spirit.
I believe that your divine Son became man
and died for our sins and that he will come
to judge the living and the dead.
I believe these and all the truths
which the Holy Catholic Church teaches
because you have revealed them
who are eternal truth and wisdom,
who can neither deceive nor be deceived.
In this faith I intend to live and die.
Amen.

Leader: We ask the assistance of the holy angels in bringing our loved ones back to the Faith.

All: Angel of God, my guardian dear, to whom God's love commits me here. Ever this day be at my side, to light and guard, to rule and guide. Amen.

OPTIONAL PERSONAL PRAYER
Prayer for Peace
Attributed to Saint Francis of Assisi
Lord, make me an instrument of your
       peace,
Where there is hatred, let me sow love;
Where there is injury, pardon;
Where there is doubt, faith;
Where there is despair, hope;
Where there is darkness, light;
Where there is sadness, joy.

O Divine Master,
Grant that I may not so much seek
To be consoled as to console;
To be understood as to understand;
To be loved as to love.

For it is in giving that we receive;
It is in pardoning that we are pardoned;
And it is in dying that we are born to
eternal life.
Amen.

THE TWELFTH STATION

Jesus Dies upon the Cross

Leader: The Twelfth Station: Jesus Dies upon the Cross

(Genuflect)

We adore you, O Christ, and we praise you …

All: Because by your holy Cross you have redeemed the world.

(Stand)

Leader: We hear in the Sacred Scriptures:

> After this Jesus, knowing that all was now finished, said (to fulfil the Scripture), "I thirst." A bowl full of vinegar stood there; so they put a sponge full of the vinegar on hyssop and held it to his mouth. When Jesus had received the vinegar, he said, "It is finished"; and he bowed his head and gave up his spirit. (John 19:28–30)

Leader: Let us pray. Lord Jesus, after the brutality of your journey to Golgotha, you have come to this pivotal point. Here at Calvary, you fulfill the reason for which you were born and the mission for which you were sent. You are Priest, Altar, and Sacrifice. Here on this prophetic hill, you freely offer yourself as the new and eternal holocaust. Your Sacrifice ends the rule of sin and death. It frees us from our ancient slavery to darkness and allows us to love and worship God without fear. As you hung upon the Cross, you saw the birth of your kingdom. You saw all of humanity, for all time, and you declared: "I thirst!" Yes, Lord, you thirst for us. You thirst for our love and for our surrender to your mercy. And you especially thirst for those who have fallen away from you. Help us to see the power and beauty of your love, which is so selfless and willing to suffer so much evil for our eternal good. Strengthen us, Lord, to see your love, poured out and crucified for us.

Lord Jesus, our loved ones do not trust

in your Cross. They seek to save themselves through the vanity, pride, power, and pleasure of our fallen world. They do not look upon your Cross, and so they cannot find you, the Savior they need. Lord, you laid down everything you had for our good. You held nothing back. You showed by your words and deeds how trustworthy you are and how reliable is the salvation you offer us. You died as an eternal holocaust of love. You died as our friend. You died as an expiation for our sins. And the oblation you offer is unsurpassable in merit and without equal in all of creation. The All-Holy, All-Powerful, and All-Knowing God has died for us. Lord, we repent of our sins and we turn to you. In our hearts, we ask you: Please, bring our loved ones back to you. Give them the grace to trust in you and to seek your fellowship in all they do. Bring them back to your Church.

(Kneel)

All: Lord, in your torturous crucifixion, you

revealed a heart that is meek and humble. In your work of salvation, you did not rule as a distant king, or triumph as a victorious general, or control as a successful man of business. In contrast to the fallenness of our world and the things it values, you came as a lowly servant. You were rejected. Your Sacrifice was mocked. You came to your own, and your own refused you. And yet, you continued to pour yourself out in service and compassion, even to those who hurt and ignored you. Lord, your Sacrifice changed the world. It brought hope to a world in darkness. It replaced tension with peace. It changed slaves into sons and daughters. In our pride, we have not fully acknowledged your Sacrifice. We have not thanked you. We have not followed your way of love. We have allowed sin and self-ishness to eclipse your Sacrifice.

Lord, we ask you to help us. We turn to you. We see your goodness and the righteousness of your Sacrifice. We thank you and praise you. We repent of all our sins. Strengthen us to love as you love. Convert our hearts! Open them to those who hurt us. Help us die to our pride. Lord, please bring our loved ones back to you and to your Church!

(Stand)

All: Our Father …

Leader: We pray an Act of Faith for ourselves and our loved ones.

All: O my God, I firmly believe
that you are one God in three divine Persons,
Father, Son, and Holy Spirit.
I believe that your divine Son became man
and died for our sins and that he will come
to judge the living and the dead.
I believe these and all the truths
which the Holy Catholic Church teaches
because you have revealed them
who are eternal truth and wisdom,
who can neither deceive nor be deceived.
In this faith I intend to live and die.
Amen.

Leader: We ask the assistance of the holy angels in bringing our loved ones back to the Faith.

All: Angel of God, my guardian dear, to whom God's love commits me here. Ever this day be at my side, to light and guard, to rule and guide. Amen.

OPTIONAL PERSONAL PRAYER
Prayer Before a Crucifix

Look down upon me, good and gentle
    Jesus,
while before Your face I humbly kneel
    and,
with burning soul,
pray and beseech You
to fix deep in my heart lively sentiments
of faith, hope and charity;
true contrition for my sins,
and a firm purpose of amendment.
While I contemplate,
with great love and tender pity,
Your five most precious wounds,
pondering over them within me

and calling to mind the words which David,
Your prophet, said of You, my Jesus:
"They have pierced My hands and My feet,
they have numbered all My bones."
Amen.

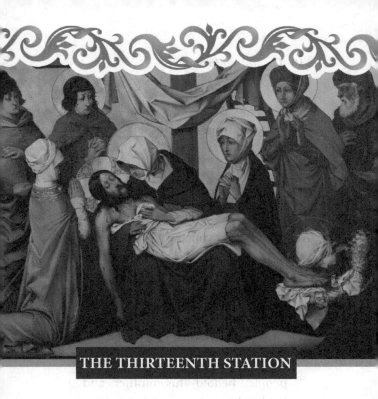

THE THIRTEENTH STATION

Jesus Is Taken Down from the Cross

Leader: The Thirteenth Station: Jesus Is Taken Down from the Cross

(Genuflect)

We adore you, O Christ, and we praise you …

All: Because by your holy Cross you have redeemed the world.

(Stand)

Leader: We hear in the Sacred Scriptures:

> While he was still speaking to the people, behold, his mother and his brethren stood outside, asking to speak to him. But he replied to the man who told him, "Who is my mother, and who are my brethren?" And stretching out his hand toward his disciples, he said, "Here are my mother and my brethren! For whoever does the will of my Father in heaven is my brother,

and sister, and mother." (Matthew
12:46–50)

Leader: Let us pray. Lord Jesus, after your
Sacrifice was complete, you were taken
down from the Cross. You were placed in
the arms of your mother, who was there
and who suffered with you. Your Sacrifice
was offered. Your oblation was complete, as
you had declared: "It is finished." And now,
you call all men and women to your sacred
fellowship. You offer salvation to each of us.
You have shown us the path of peace and
the most excellent way of love. You invite
us to follow you. The summons stands at
the door of each of our hearts. You knock
and wait.

Lord Jesus, our loved ones suffer a thou-
sand crosses that cannot save them. They
do not accept the merits of your redeeming
Cross. They are distracted and are far from
you. They are choosing their own way, and
it is hurting them. It is hurting their fellowship with you. Without your way of peace
and love, our fallenness chooses the lower

things of this world. We replace tranquility with domination and love with selfishness. Without you as our model and source of grace, we stray from the path of goodness and selfless service. We get lost and become stuck in our own pride. But you, Lord, have given everything. You were placed in the arms of your mother as a dead man. There was nothing left to give. Your Sacrifice and generosity of heart call to us all. They summon and invite everyone to come, see, accept, and follow your way of love and eternal salvation. Lord, we need you. Our loved ones need you. They are dead people walking without grace or spiritual purpose. Please bring them back to you. Give them the grace to trust in you and seek your fellowship in all they do. Bring them back to your Church.

(Kneel)

All: Lord, you completed the mission given to you. You remained focused and tenacious. You allowed nothing to distract you. You only sought to do the will of the Father in everything. As you were taken down from the Cross, you were placed in the arms of your mother. After a torturous Passion, you were finally able to rest in the arms of your mother. She was your first disciple, faithful to the will of God in all things. From your incarnation at the words of the Archangel Gabriel, to the brutality of your Passion, your mother trusted in the will of the Father. She surrendered her entire life to this task, as she announced: "Behold, I am the handmaid of the Lord; let it be done to me according to your word." Lord, help us to be a true mother, brother, and sister to you. Strengthen us to know the will of the Father and to accomplish it generously. Guide our hearts to a joyful obedience to you in all things. Take away our compromises, excuses, and denials. Have mercy on us and bless us.

Lord, help us. We need you. You bring life from death. Please give us rebirth. Lift up our hearts. Heal us from the wounds of our pride. Give us a strong faith, a sturdy

hope, and a selfless love. We trust in you.
Please bring our loved ones back to you and
to your Church!

(Stand)

All: Our Father …

Leader: We pray an Act of Faith for ourselves and our loved ones.

All: O my God, I firmly believe
that you are one God in three divine Persons,
Father, Son, and Holy Spirit.
I believe that your divine Son became man
and died for our sins and that he will come
to judge the living and the dead.
I believe these and all the truths
which the Holy Catholic Church teaches
because you have revealed them
who are eternal truth and wisdom,
who can neither deceive nor be deceived.
In this faith I intend to live and die.
Amen.

Leader: We ask the assistance of the holy angels in bringing our loved ones back to the Faith.

All: Angel of God, my guardian dear, to whom God's love commits me here. Ever this day be at my side, to light and guard, to rule and guide. Amen.

OPTIONAL PERSONAL PRAYER
Mary's Song of Praise ("Magnificat")
Luke 1:46–55

My soul magnifies the Lord,
and my spirit rejoices in God my Savior,
for he has regarded the low estate of his
    handmaiden.
For behold, henceforth all generations
    will call me blessed;
for he who is mighty has done great
    things for me,
and holy is his name.
And his mercy is on those who fear him
from generation to generation.
He has shown strength with his arm,

he has scattered the proud in the imagi-
   nation of their hearts,
he has put down the mighty from their
   thrones,
and exalted those of low degree;
he has filled the hungry with good
   things,
and the rich he has sent empty away.
   He has helped his servant Israel,
in remembrance of his mercy,
as he spoke to our fathers,
to Abraham and to his posterity forever.

Jesus Is Laid in the Tomb

Leader: The Fourteenth Station: Jesus Is Laid in the Tomb

(Genuflect)

We adore you, O Christ, and we praise you …

All: Because by your holy Cross you have redeemed the world.

(Stand)

Leader: We hear in the Sacred Scriptures:

> When it was evening, there came a rich man from Arimathea, named Joseph, who also was a disciple of Jesus. He went to Pilate and asked for the body of Jesus. Then Pilate ordered it to be given to him. And Joseph took the body, and wrapped it in a clean linen shroud, and laid it in his own new tomb, which he had hewn in the rock; and he rolled a great stone to the

door of the tomb, and departed.
(Matthew 27:57–60)

Leader: Let us pray. Lord Jesus, after your death on the Cross, you were placed in the tomb. As your human body rested, your human soul went to the holding place of the great saints of the Old Testament. There you preached the Gospel and offered them salvation. Before your redeeming work, heaven was not open to us. But you came to us and freed us. You opened the gates of heaven. And you did not forget any of those who loved and served the will of your Father. Lord Jesus, you are the righteous Savior. You are the Beginning and End of all things. And you have not lost any of those entrusted to you. In spite of the infidelity of your people, you have only responded with love and faithfulness. You seek us out. You call us to yourself.

Lord Jesus, our loved ones are neglecting you. They dismiss your offer of love and salvation. They live in a tomb, without the hope of new life. They have removed themselves from the flow of your grace. Lord, as you once rested in a tomb that led to Resurrection, so rest in the hearts of our loved ones. Be with them. Lead them out of the darkness. Bring them into the radiance of your light and the splendor of your glory. Please, Lord, bring our loved ones back to you. Give them the grace to trust in you and seek your fellowship in all they do. Bring them back to your Church.

(Kneel)

All: Lord, by resting in the tomb, you displayed your desire to rest in our hearts. You ask to be the constant Guest and Lord of our souls. You offer us a life of love, mercy, and compassion. Help us to follow you. From the tomb, you give us hope. You conquer sin and death. And you offer us not only the joys of heaven, but an abundant life in this world. Help us to accept this newness of life. Save us. As you knew coldness from the death of your human body, spare us from the coldness of our fallen world. As your body suffered all the consequences of death, save us from the emptiness of sin. Convert us. Show us the beauty and power of a life lived in you. Lord, you are the firstborn of a new creation. You are the Good Shepherd. You are the Savior and Redeemer. Come to us. Help us. In our own hurt and coldness of heart, we have not given a strong witness to your abundant life. We have weakened the power of your testimony to those who are away from you. We need your help.

Lord, come to us! Convert us! Open our hearts to live the fullness of life you promise. Strengthen us to be instruments of your peace and witnesses to your love. Save us, Lord. Save our loved ones who are away from you. Bring your warmth to cold hearts. Bring our loved ones back to you and to your Church!

(Stand)

All: Our Father …

Leader: We pray an Act of Faith for ourselves and our loved ones.

All: O my God, I firmly believe
that you are one God in three divine Persons,
Father, Son, and Holy Spirit.
I believe that your divine Son became man
and died for our sins and that he will come
to judge the living and the dead.
I believe these and all the truths
which the Holy Catholic Church teaches
because you have revealed them
who are eternal truth and wisdom,
who can neither deceive nor be deceived.
In this faith I intend to live and die.
Amen.

Leader: We ask the assistance of the holy
angels in bringing our loved ones back to
the Faith.

All: Angel of God, my guardian dear, to
whom God's love commits me here. Ever
this day be at my side, to light and guard, to
rule and guide. Amen.

OPTIONAL PERSONAL PRAYER
Serenity Prayer
God, grant me the serenity
to accept the things I cannot change;
courage to change the things I can;
and wisdom to know the difference.

Living one day at a time;
enjoying one moment at a time;
accepting hardships as
the pathway to peace;
taking, as He did, this sinful world
as it is, not as I would have it;
trusting that He will make all things right
if I surrender to His Will;
that I may be reasonably happy in this life
and supremely happy with Him
forever in the next.
Amen.

Closing Prayer

Leader: In the Name of the Father, and of the Son, and of the Holy Spirit. Amen.

Lord Jesus, you are the Resurrection and the Life.

You suffered for our salvation and you labored for our redemption. You walked the bitter way of the Cross and held nothing back. You loved us to the end. You are the loving Savior and the compassionate

Redeemer.

In the way of the Cross, you manifested your passionate love for us. You showed yourself to be Our Lord, Good Shepherd, and Older Brother. You proved the truthfulness of your heart and the trustworthiness of your promises.

In carrying the Cross, you endured bitterness, injury, and mockery. You humbly accepted all of these mistreatments, so that light could scatter darkness and life could come from death. You won an eternal life for us in heaven, as you also won for us an abundant life here and now.

Lord, we thank you, and we seek the help of your grace. Help us to follow your way. Guide us to accept the sufferings of this world and to always let good triumph.

Lord, today we walked the way of the Cross for our loved ones who have fallen away from you. Our hearts are broken and confused. We grieve that they have left your fellowship and the practice of the Faith. We pray for their return.

Lord, as the way of your Cross leads us

to bold confidence in your Resurrection, so we have bold confidence that your grace will convert loved ones, bringing them back to you and to your Church.

We surrender them to you. Please help them!

Lord, use the grace of this sorrowful way to bring them back.

Lord Jesus, we trust in you!

In the Name of the Father, and of the Son, and of the Holy Spirit. Amen.

Additional Spiritual Resources

In addition to the Stations of the Cross, the spiritual treasury of the Church has a vast array of spiritual resources that can be used to intercede for our loved ones who have left the practice of the Faith. Some of the suggestions below are more applicable to specific cultures within the Church, but all of them are offered here and can be used at your discretion. Each of the resources below has been proven reliable by the lived tradition of the Church. They are excellent resources during the slow, and oftentimes painful, process of bringing loved ones back to the Lord Jesus and his Church.

Here are a few suggestions:

Mass Intentions. Consider having a Mass offered for your loved ones. These can be offered any day, but birthdays and anniversaries are often a nice option. Depending on the openness of the loved one, you might send them a Mass card, but this is not necessary. In the end, the real power is in the offering of the Mass and the assistance of its grace.

Adoration. Prayers offered before the Lord Jesus truly present in the Blessed Sacrament are particularly powerful. Saints throughout the Christian tradition have encouraged supplication and intercession offered before the Blessed Sacrament. You might spend time in adoration praying for the return of your loved ones, as this can be a tremendous source of grace. In addition, depending on how open your loved ones are, you might consider inviting them to join you in adoration (which they might see as simply "quiet prayer"). For many who have left the Church, an invitation to adoration is easier to accept than an invitation to come to Mass. For some, the idea of Mass can be overwhelming, but adoration might seem less intimidating as a first step. Depending on your loved one, consider extending an invitation to adoration and see what happens.

Rosary. Pray a decade of the Rosary — or even a full Rosary! — for your loved one(s). This can be done daily or on a specific day of the week. This can also be done before a conversation or interaction with the loved one. Any of the Joyful, Sorrowful, Luminous, or Glorious mysteries could be prayed, but the Sorrowful Mysteries might resonate more with the suffering of the situation.

Divine Mercy Chaplet. While the Divine Mercy Chaplet is a comparatively newer devotion, it has already proven itself to be spiritually powerful. You might pray a decade of the chaplet, or the full chaplet, for your loved one's conversion and return to the practice of the Faith.

Novenas to Specific Saints. The Church offers a vast multitude of novenas to various saints. Any of these nine-day prayer devotions can be of spiritual assistance, especially to saints who have a tie to our loved one. You might consider finding out their namesake, their Confirmation saint, the saint of their birthday, or the patron of their occupation. By choosing a saint that is somehow connected to your loved one, you might find more of a spiritual connection and a greater consolation in making the novena.

Green Scapular. The Green Scapular of the Immaculate Heart of Mary has consistently been associated with the graces of conversion. In particular, we seek these graces for those who have left the Faith. You can wear the Green Scapular for the conversion of a loved one and/or place the scapular on (or behind) their picture.

Miraculous Medal. The Miraculous Medal, formally known as the Medal of the Immaculate Conception, is also associated with the graces of conversion. You can wear the medal for a loved one, or leave it discreetly in the loved one's home or car. The latter practice should be considered only after serious discernment, and it is very important not to do this in a spirit of superstition.

Prayers to Saint Monica. For over a decade of her life, Saint Monica persevered in prayer and hope for the conversion of her son. In time, he did convert, and today we know him as Saint Augustine. In honor of her tenacity in this spiritual work, Saint Monica is a patron of those who have fallen away from the Faith. As such, she is a specific friend to us and an intercessor we can rely on in our spiritual efforts to bring our loved ones back to the Faith.

Prayers to Patron Saints. In addition to Saint Monica, we can also turn to other saints who are patrons of other issues that might be related to why our loved ones left the Church. For example, Saint Helena for the divorced; Saint Maximilian Kolbe for those fighting drug addictions; Saint Faustina for those stuck in unforgiveness; Saint Dymphna for those struggling with emotional or mental disorders; and Saint Charles Lwanga for those with same-sex attractions.

The above are only a few additional options from the Church's spiritual treasury. Whatever practice or devotion you use, your efforts should always focus on God's grace and his providential care for us. In our prayers for our loved ones, we must avoid any semblance of superstition — thinking that an object or practice has power by itself. All spiritual power comes from God alone. Certain spiritual practices or devotional items have been blessed by God, and can therefore become a means by which his grace can work. But it is always God working through a blessed practice or devotional item, and never the practice or item by itself.

Talking with Our Loved Ones

When a loved one leaves the Church or totally abandons the Christian faith, it can cause us deep distress. Sometimes, our own responses, actions, and reactions surprise us. Some of us may have used guilt or shame, while others chose to alienate or ceaselessly nag a loved one. But such approaches, and others like them, are never helpful in bringing loved ones back to the Church.

In this book, we focused on a spiritual response. Such a response should always be first and foremost in our minds and hearts. But while such a response is primary, it is not exclusive. We should always leave doors open for conversation.

Anyone who has left the Church should know that we are willing and ready to talk and listen. In addition, we should prudently choose times to respectfully initiate conversation about the Faith.

In such conversations, it's good to have some help. A mental outline or structure for a conversation can be of great assistance. To that end, here is a suggested three-part process for any conversation:

- Actively listen when people are speaking. Desire to understand what they are saying, where they are coming from, and what is in their hearts.

- Look for ideas and convictions
  that you share with the other
  person.
- Use what you have in com-
  mon with the other person as
  a bridge for dialogue.

Even if the discussion leads to debate and
disagreement, it should always by marked
by greater unity and deeper respect. This
approach shouldn't surprise us, since it
is the very one that Jesus Christ lived and
modeled for us.

This approach to dialogue moves us
beyond judgments and offensive approaches, helping us to truly engage those who are
struggling with their faith or with aspects
of the Catholic Church. This approach also
reminds us that inviting someone back
to the Church shouldn't be a contest or a
battle of wills; it should be a truly human
outreach that desires the good of the other
person and seeks to give witness to Jesus
Christ and his Church.

In the end, this approach exemplifies

the maxim of the Christian spiritual tradition: "Heart speaks to heart." When believers listen to the heart of another, and encompass it with sincere prayer, miraculous and surprising things can happen.

Bibliography

Baker, Robert. *The Questioner's Prayer.* Huntington, IN: Our Sunday Visitor, 2007.

Champlin, Joseph. *The Stations of the Cross with Pope John Paul II.* Liguori, MO: Liguori Publications, 1994.

Enzler, Clarence. *Everyone's Way of the Cross.* Notre Dame, IN: Ave Maria Press, 2014.

Furey, Richard G. *Mary's Way of the Cross.*
  Mystic, CT: Twenty-Third Publications, 1984.

Niba, Herbert. *The Way of the Cross with St.
  John Paul II.* Huntington, IN: Our Sunday Visitor, 2019.

Sheen, Fulton. *The Way of the Cross.* New
  York: Saint Paul's Press, 2019.

Tassone, Susan. *The Way of the Cross for the
  Holy Souls in Purgatory.* Huntington,
  IN: Our Sunday Visitor, 2005.

Watkins, James. *Manual of Prayers.* Chica-
  go: Midwest Theological Forum, 1998.

About the Author

Father Jeffrey Kirby, STD, is a Papal Missionary of Mercy and the pastor of Our Lady of Grace Parish in Indian Land, South Carolina. He is an adjunct professor of theology at Belmont Abbey College, and regularly speaks about God's mercy and evangelization at conferences and retreats throughout the United States.